California
The Golden State

Tika Downey

PowerKiDS
press™

New York

Published in 2010 by The Rosen Publishing Group, Inc.
29 East 21st Street, New York, NY 10010

First Edition

Editor: Joanne Randolph
Book Design: Greg Tucker
Photo Researcher: Jessica Gerweck

Photo Credits: Cover, p. 5, 22 (flag), 22 (flower) Shutterstock.com; p. 7 © Philip James Corwin/Corbis; p. 9 © Bettmann/Corbis; pp. 17, 24 (John Muir), 24 (Tiger Woods) Getty Images; p. 11 © Richard T. Nowitz/Corbis; p. 13 Nash Photos/Getty Images; p. 15 (main) Robert Glusic/Getty Images; p. 15 (inset) © Louie Psihoyos/Corbis; p. 19 Gavin Hellier/Robert Harding World Imagery/Corbis; p. 22 (tree) © www.istockphoto.com/Bill Grove; p. 22 (animal) © www.istockphoto.com/Linda Mirro; p. 22 (bird) © www.istockphoto.com/Laure Neish; p. 22 (Sally Ride) Time & Life Pictures/Getty Images.

Library of Congress Cataloging-in-Publication Data

Downey, Tika.
  California : the Golden State / Tika Downey. — 1st ed.
      p. cm. — (Our amazing states)
  Includes bibliographical references and index.
  ISBN 978-1-4042-8110-3 (library binding) — ISBN 978-1-4358-3340-1 (pbk.) —
ISBN 978-1-4358-3341-8 (6-pack)
  1. California—Juvenile literature. I. Title.
  F861.3.D69 2010
  979.4—dc22
                                                2009000543

Manufactured in the United States of America

Contents

The Golden State

You have likely heard of California. Almost everyone has. It is a big state on the West Coast. Only two states are bigger than California, and more people live in California than in any other state.

California is **famous** because Hollywood is there. Movies and TV shows are made in this part of Los Angeles. Many people also come to California to visit Disneyland, a big park with lots of rides and fun things to do. California also has high mountains, giant **redwood** trees, and beautiful beaches.

California first became famous when gold was discovered on the American River, near Sacramento, in 1848. Thousands of people rushed there to look for gold. That is how California got its nickname, the Golden State.

This sign in Hollywood Hills, California, has come to stand for California's movie and TV business. First built in 1923, the sign said Hollywoodland until 1949.

Long Ago in California

California's first people were Native Americans. The earliest ones may have arrived 25,000 years ago! By around 1540, there were about 300,000 Native Americans living in California.

The first Europeans to see California were Spanish **explorers**, led by Juan Rodríguez Cabrillo. They sailed along the coast in 1542. Beginning in 1769, the Spanish founded **presidios**, **missions**, and settlements in California.

Spain ruled California until 1822, when Mexico took control of it. The first U.S. settlers reached California in 1841. By 1846, there were lots of U.S. settlers in California, and they wanted to be free from Mexico.

This is the Mission San Diego de Alcalá, in San Diego, which was built in 1769. This was the first of 21 missions built in California that were all about a day's walk away from each other.

The Thirty-first State

In 1846, some U.S. settlers in California announced that California was a free **republic**. They took over the main Mexican presidio and put up a flag with a star, a bear, and the words "California Republic" on it. This became known as the Bear Flag **Revolt**.

The United States gained control of California in 1848, after it won a war with Mexico. The discovery of gold that same year started the gold rush. People from around the world hurried to California hoping to get rich. The population quickly grew from about 15,000 to about 100,000. In 1850, California became the thirty-first state.

In this picture, people are panning for gold in a California river. The people who came to California looking for gold were called Forty-niners.

Mountains, Valleys, and Deserts

What kind of land do you picture when you think of California? This large state has many types of land.

There are mountains in California, such as the Coast **Ranges** in the west and the Sierra Nevada in the east. Between the Coast Ranges and the Sierra Nevada is the Central Valley. This green valley has rich soil that is good for farming. East of the Sierra Nevada is a huge desert area called the Great Basin. The Mojave Desert and Death Valley are part of the Great Basin. Death Valley has the lowest land in all of North America! It is also the driest, hottest place in North America.

Here you can see Half Dome, a famous mountain in Yosemite National Park, on the left. The park is in the Sierra Nevada.

The Wild Side

California is often warm and sunny. However, it also has fog, rain, and even snow. The Sierra Nevada can get more than 37 feet (11 m) of snow yearly!

More than 40,000 kinds of animals and plants live in California. The state's animals include coyotes, rattlesnakes, bighorn sheep, beavers, and North America's largest bird, the California condor.

California has desert cacti and large forests. California redwoods are the world's tallest trees. Some are more than 300 feet (90 m) tall! Did you know that redwoods can live for centuries? Some are over 1,500 years old!

This girl looks up at a California redwood in California's Redwood National Park. In 2008, the tallest-known tree in the world was a 378-foot (115 m) redwood in that park.

California Business

Did you know that California produces more goods and services than most countries in the world? It is true! Californian businesses make computers, airplanes, and many sorts of tools and machines. The state is also an important center for movies, TV, and the music business.

More than half of the United States' fruits and vegetables are grown in California. Grapes, strawberries, oranges, tomatoes, lettuce, and carrots grow there. Almonds and walnuts are also important crops from California.

California makes lots of money from people who vacation there. About 250 million people visit California yearly! Would you like to go?

California's grapes are used to make products such as wine and raisins. *Inset:* California is home to many movie and TV studios, such as Paramount Pictures, shown here.

California's Capital

Sacramento began as a small settlement in 1839. It grew quickly after gold was discovered nearby in 1848. It became California's capital in 1854.

Today, visitors can see buildings built during the days of the gold rush. They can go to the Crocker Art **Museum**, the West's oldest art museum. They can learn about Sacramento's past at the California State Historic Railroad Museum. Did you know that the West's first railroad ran between Sacramento and Folsom, California? Did you know that Sacramento was also the western end of the first coast-to-coast railroad? Sacramento has a lot for you to see and do!

This is Sacramento's capitol building, which was built between 1860 and 1874. This building serves as a museum and as the working seat of California's government.

The Bridge at the Golden Gate

San Francisco, in northern California, has one of the world's most famous and beautiful bridges, the Golden Gate Bridge. The bright orange bridge opened in 1937. It draws about nine million visitors each year.

Like most people, you may wonder how the bridge got its name. The bridge gets its name from the **strait** it crosses, the Golden Gate Strait. You might think the strait was named for the goldfields nearby, but that is not true. John Frémont, a famous mapmaker and explorer, gave the strait its name because it reminded him of another harbor he knew, called the Golden Horn.

The Golden Gate Bridge is about 1.7 miles (2.7 km) long and its towers are 746 feet (227 m) tall. Its bright orange color helps ships see the bridge on foggy days.

A Great Place to Visit

Visitors can find all sorts of things to do in California. You can visit deserts, beaches, or giant redwood forests. You can go to Disneyland or SeaWorld. You can visit San Francisco and the Golden Gate Bridge. You can visit Los Angeles and Hollywood. Maybe you can take a surfing lesson or visit the famous sea lions on San Francisco's **Pier** 39.

In Los Angeles, you can also see the famous La Brea Tar Pits, where thick, sticky oil forms pools on the ground. Thousands of years ago, animals got trapped in the tar pits and died. You can see **fossils** from the animals at a museum there. What would you like to do in California?

Glossary

explorers (ek-SPLOR-urz) People who travel and look for new land.

famous (FAY-mus) Well known.

fossils (FAH-sulz) Hardened remains of dead animals or plants.

missions (MIH-shunz) Places where church leaders teach their beliefs and help the community.

museum (myoo-ZEE-um) A place where art or historical pieces are safely kept for people to see and to study.

pier (PEER) A deck, built out over water, at which boats can dock.

presidios (preh-SEE-dee-ohz) Spanish forts, usually built to protect nearby missions.

ranges (RAYN-juz) Rows of mountains.

redwood (RED-wood) A very tall tree that produces cones with seeds.

republic (rih-PUH-blik) A form of government in which the people elect representatives who run the government.

revolt (rih-VOLT) A fight against the authority of a government.

strait (STRAYT) A narrow waterway connecting two larger bodies of water.

California State Symbols

State Tree
California
Redwood

State Animal
California Grizzly
Bear

State Flag

State Bird
California Valley
Quail

State Flower
Golden Poppy

State Seal

Famous People From California

John Muir
(1838-1914)
Born in Scotland
(moved to CA in 1868),
Naturalist/Preservationist

Sally Ride
(1951–)
Born in Los Angeles, CA
Astronaut/Physicist/
First Woman in Space

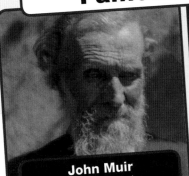
Tiger Woods
(1975–)
Born in Cypress, CA
Professional Golfer

California State Map

Legend

○ Major City

✪ Capital

〜 River

Klamath Mountains

Cascade Mountains

Goose Lake

Sacramento River

Coast Range

Lake Tahoe

○ Napa

✪ Sacramento

San Francisco ○ ○ Oakland

○ San Jose

Sierra Nevada

San Joaquin River

Fresno ○

Death Valley

Coast Range

Channel Islands

○ Los Angeles

San Bernardino ○

○ Palm Springs

Mojave Desert

Santa Catalina

Salton Sea

Colorado River

San Clemente

○ San Diego

California State Facts

Population: About 36,553,215

Area: About 158,706 square miles (411,047 sq km)

Motto: Eureka! (I Have Found It!)

Song: "I Love You, California," words by F. B. Silverwood and music by A. F. Frankenstein

Index

Web Sites

Due to the changing nature of Internet links, PowerKids Press has developed an online list of Web sites related to the subject of this book. This site is updated regularly. Please use this link to access the list:
www.powerkidslinks.com/amst/ca/